Contents

A country childhood

Isaac Newton was born on Christmas Day in 1642. His father, a farmer, had died three months earlier. When his mother remarried, she left her son Isaac to be brought up by his grandparents at Woolsthorpe Manor.

Woolsthorpe Manor in Lincolnshire, Isaac's childhood home.

Oct 1642

Civil war breaks out in England.

1642

Isaac Newton is born.

1646

His mother marries again, to Barnabas Smith.

ISAAC NEWTON

Sarah Ridley

W

FRANKLIN WATTS
LONDON • SYDNEY

Franklin Watts

Published in Great Britain in 2017 by
The Watts Publishing Group

Editor in Chief: John C. Miles
Design: Jonathan Hair and Matt Lilly
Art Director: Peter Scoulding
Picture Research: Diana Morris
Original design concept: Sophie Williams

Picture credits: BAL/Getty Images: 20. Robert Bird/Alamy: 9.
CC © Cambridge University Library: front cover bg, 10.
John P Carr/Alamy: 5. Cmglee/CC/Wikimedia Commons: 7.
Celso Diniz/Dreamstime: 23. duncan1890/istockphoto: front cover c.
Werner Forman/Getty Images: 22. Fritzbruno/CC/Wikimedia
Commons: 6. The Granger Collection/Topfoto: 8, 14. Image Asset
Management/Superstock: 4. David G. Johnson: front cover t. Lebrecht
Music & Arts PL/Alamy: 1, 2, 17. NASA/JPL/Caltech: front cover tr.
David Parker/SPL: 11. Piero/CC/Wikimedia Commons: 18. © The
Royal Society: 21. SPL: 16. Richard Valencia/© The Royal Society: 12.
CC/Wikimedia Commons: 13, 15. World History Archive/Topfoto: 19.

Dewey number: 530'.092
ISBN 978 1 4451 5360 5

Printed in China

Franklin Watts
An imprint of Hachette Children's Group
Part of The Watts Publishing Group
Carmelite House, 50 Victoria Embankment
London EC4Y 0DZ

An Hachette UK Company

www.hachette.co.uk
www.franklinwatts.co.uk

FSC
www.fsc.org
MIX
Paper from
responsible sources
FSC® C104740

1642–1653

Re-enactors stage one of the battles fought during the English Civil War.

England was a difficult place to live at this time. Groups of people around the country were fighting each other in a civil war. At home in the countryside, Isaac spent a lot of time on his own, experimenting with sundials and shadow clocks.

1649

King Charles I is executed.

1650

Isaac becomes a pupil at the local school.

1653

His mother returns to Woolsthorpe with her children after the death of her husband.

School to university

At the local grammar school Isaac's teachers gradually realised he was very clever. His mother, however, wanted him to run the family farm and she took him out of school when he was 17. Isaac was no good at farming so he returned to school and prepared to go to Trinity College, Cambridge.

Isaac went to King's School, Grantham, where you can still see his name, carved into a windowsill.

1655–1665

Much of Trinity College was built around a hundred years before Isaac's birth.

At university, Isaac followed his interests in maths, physics, astronomy and the science of sight and light. To fund his student life he had to act as a servant for wealthier students. During this time he made a list of questions that he wanted to answer.

The falling apple

An outbreak of plague closed the university in 1665. Isaac Newton returned to the safety of his childhood home. Here he spent the next two years, reading books about science and focusing on complicated maths problems.

So many people died from plague in 1665 that in London victims had to be buried in mass graves.

1665–1666

In London, 100,000 people die of the plague.

1665–1667

Isaac spends time working out how to use maths to calculate the rate of change of moving objects or changing temperatures. It is called calculus (see page 21 for more on this).

He fills notebooks with his ideas about gravity.

1665-1667

As an old man, Isaac told the story of how a falling apple at Woolsthorpe Manor inspired his ideas about gravity.

One day, Isaac was sitting under an apple tree when an apple fell to the ground. He started to wonder about the invisible force that made the apple fall to the ground. Did this same force hold the whole universe together?

BREAKTHROUGH

Isaac went on to prove with maths that the same force that pulled an apple to the ground held the Moon in orbit around the Earth and the planets of the solar system in orbit around the Sun. This force is called gravity.

Light and sight

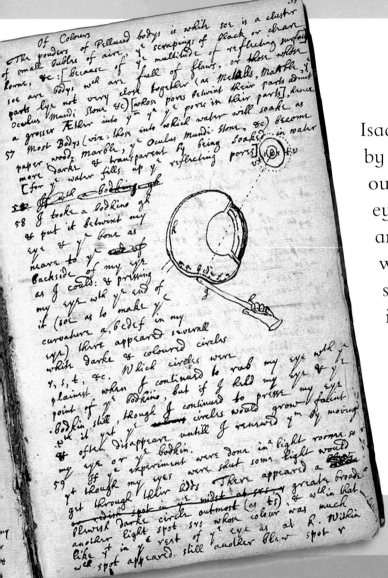

Isaac also became fascinated by light and sight, carrying out experiments on his own eyes. He stared at the Sun and then looked at a blank wall, noting down that he saw circles of colour. To investigate how the eye sees, he poked a long needle, called a bodkin, into his own eye.

Isaac's sketch of his experiment with the bodkin.

1665–1667

Isaac carries out many experiments with colour and light.	He puts his own eyesight in danger by experimenting on himself.	He does not publish any of his ideas but keeps careful written notes. He repeats experiments time and time again.	He reads *Micrographia* by Robert Hooke (see page 13).

He experimented with light, using prisms. He made the room dark and allowed a beam of sunlight to pass through a prism. Then he set up a second prism to catch some of the beams of coloured light that had been split by the first prism. Each beam of coloured light kept its colour – and did not split again. This proved that white light is actually made up of colours.

EXPERIMENT

On a sunny day you can split light to see its rainbow colours using a glass of water. Place the glass on a piece of white paper and watch the sunlight pass through the water in the glass and split into rainbow colours.

Isaac showed that the prism did not add colour to light – it split white light into colours.

The pocket telescope

After two years, it was safe for Isaac to return to his studies at Cambridge University. At this time he invented a reflecting telescope, using mirrors as well as lenses. It was pocket-sized but it magnified as well as a telescope ten times its length.

The pocket telescope was small enough to be carried about on board ship.

1667–1672

Members of the Royal Society were very impressed by the pocket telescope and invited Isaac to join their society. At this time, Isaac decided to publish his work on light and colour. When an important member of the Royal Society, Robert Hooke, criticised the work, Isaac was furious.

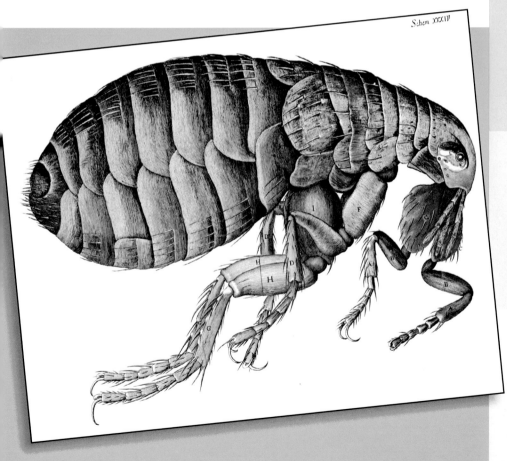

A flea from Micrographia, *Robert Hooke's book of drawings made using a microscope.*

1667

Isaac returns to university.

1668

He is awarded an MA, a further degree.

1669

He becomes a professor of maths.

1671

His pocket telescope is shown to members of the Royal Society.

1672

He becomes a member of the Royal Society.

He publishes his work on light and colour.

13

Alchemy and magic

Isaac hated criticism and found it hard to get on with people. After the argument with Robert Hooke he returned to Cambridge and shut himself away from people for about 12 years. In secret he was carrying out experiments, searching for the way to turn ordinary metals into gold and silver.

For hundreds of years alchemists searched for magical potions to extend life and to turn metals into gold and silver.

The only person who knew of these experiments was his assistant. Isaac kept his careful notes hidden, alongside notes he made about the Bible and religion. Among other ideas, he tried to work out when the Earth was created by studying the Bible.

BREAKTHROUGH

Isaac was one of the first people to work as scientists do today – taking an idea and testing it by repeating experiments. In his secret work searching for gold he did not get the result he was looking for, but he recorded his attempts to do so.

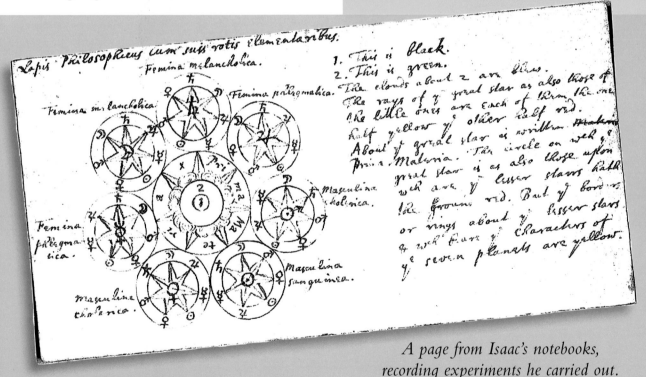

A page from Isaac's notebooks, recording experiments he carried out.

1672–1684	1679	1680–1681
Isaac studies alchemy, as well as the Bible.	His mother dies.	He exchanges letters about comets with John Flamsteed.

His great idea

1684

Edmond Halley visits Isaac.

1684

Gottfried Leibniz publishes his work on calculus (see page 21).

Edmond Halley was an astronomer and mathematician.

1686

Isaac works out the maths to prove his ideas on the laws of motion and on gravity.

Isaac continued to live quietly in Cambridge until a visit from an important astronomer, Edmond Halley, made him return to some work he had done as a student. Halley wanted Isaac to help him explain the movement of the planets in the sky. All the great scientists of the day were trying to work this out.

Isaac told Halley that the planets followed the path of an ellipse (an oval shape) and that he had already worked this out 20 years earlier. For the next two years Isaac built on the work he had done as a student and improved it, writing everything down to prove his ideas.

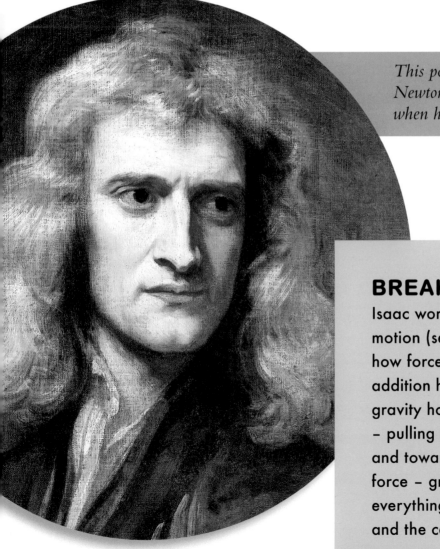

This portrait of Isaac Newton dates from 1689 when he was in his forties.

BREAKTHROUGH

Isaac worked out three laws of motion (see page 24) that explain how forces make everything move. In addition he used maths to prove that gravity holds the universe together – pulling planets towards each other and towards the Sun. This same force – gravity – pulls people and everything else towards the ground and the centre of the Earth.

Fame

Halley encouraged Isaac to publish his work, which was called *Principia Mathematica*. Those that could understand Isaac's ideas were amazed at what he had done. His ideas about universal gravity could be used to explain everything – how the universe held together, why tides rose and fell and how buildings stayed up.

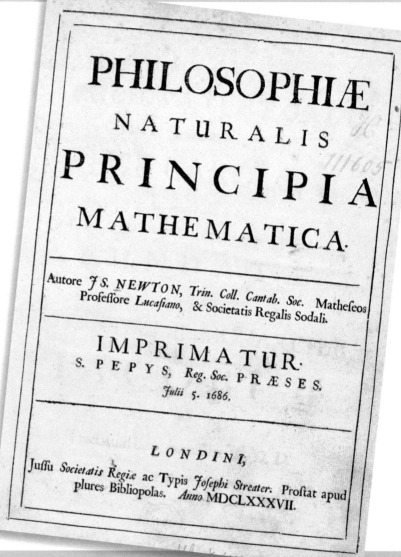

The title page of Isaac's book, which was written in Latin.

1687

Halley encourages Isaac to publish his ideas.

Isaac has a bitter argument with Robert Hooke, who claims to have done the same work on gravity.

1687–1696

Isaac became really famous – a superstar among the cleverest people of Europe. He started to spread his ideas by writing and talking about them. For the next thirty years he continued to publish and improve the work he had already done.

Isaac was a famous and wealthy man when this portrait was painted in 1702.

1692

Isaac becomes the Member of Parliament for Cambridge.

1693

He suffers a mental breakdown for six months and recovers.

1696

He leaves Cambridge to live in London.

Arise, Sir Isaac

As a reward for all of his scientific work, the government gave Isaac an important job working for the Royal Mint. He moved to London where he worked hard and was paid well. In 1703 he was elected President of the Royal Society and kept this position for the rest of his life. He was knighted in 1706.

This picture from the early 1800s shows one of the rooms where workers made coins at the Royal Mint.

1696–1699

Isaac is given the job of Warden and then Master of the Royal Mint.

1703

He is elected President of the Royal Society.

1704

Opticks – his work on colour and light – is published, along with his ideas on calculus.

1696–1726

D. ISAACVS NEWTON EQVES
REG. SOCIETATIS PRÆSES AN: 1703.

In 1712 a big argument about calculus blew up at the Royal Society. Calculus is the maths that can be used to describe things that change, such as how fast a ball is falling. Isaac felt that Gottfried Leibniz had stolen his ideas when in fact Leibniz had worked out a different version of the same thing. A vicious argument followed.

Sir Isaac donated this portrait of himself to the Royal Society in 1717.

1706

He becomes
Sir Isaac
Newton.

1712

He has a nasty
argument with Leibniz
about calculus.

1713–1726

He publishes several
improved versions of his
books, *Principia* and *Opticks*.

21

Sir Isaac's ideas live on

1727

Sir Isaac
Newton
dies.

At the age of 84, Sir Isaac Newton died at home. The government organised a huge state funeral for their great scientist and he was buried in Westminster Abbey in London.

Sir Isaac Newton's tomb in Westminster Abbey, London.

1727–today

Sir Isaac Newton is one of the greatest scientists to have ever lived. His ideas went far beyond what was already known and are still used in science today.

He invented the maths to explain his ideas and his ideas about gravity continue to help people understand how everything is held together in the universe.

People still use Newton's work to help them launch rockets into space.

Glossary

alchemy/alchemist The search for a way to turn ordinary metals into gold by people called alchemists.

astronomy/astronomer The study of the stars in the sky by experts called astronomers.

calculus The maths that can be used to describe things that change, such as a falling object.

comet An object made of ice, dust and gas that orbits the Sun.

English Civil War The period of time between 1642 and 1651 when the Parliamentarians fought supporters of King Charles I and then King Charles II.

force A push or a pull. A force changes the speed, direction or shape of an object.

grammar school In the past, a school that focused on the teaching of Latin.

gravity A force of attraction between all objects.

lens A piece of glass with curved sides used in telescopes (and other instruments) to make objects appear bigger.

magnified Increase the size of something by looking at it through a microscope or other instrument.

orbit In our solar system, the path that one heavenly body follows as it travels around another.

plague A disease that spreads easily and caused many deaths in England during 1665–1666.

Royal Society A group of scientists who met regularly to discuss the latest scientific topics from 1660 onwards, and continue to meet today.

solar system The Sun and all the objects that orbit it, including planets, asteroids and comets.

sundial A clock that uses a shadow cast by the Sun to show the time.

universe Everything that is known to exist – our solar system, the Milky Way and all the other galaxies.

Three laws of motion

1. If an object is not moving, it will not start moving by itself. So an object that is not being pushed or pulled by a force will either stay still, or keep moving in a straight line.

2. Forces make things move faster and further.

3. For every action there is an equal or opposite reaction.